Sharav

Sharav

Dvora Levin

Ekstasis Editions

Published in 2008 by:

Ekstasis Editions Canada Ltd.
Box 8474, Main Postal Outlet
Victoria, B.C. V8W 3S1

Ekstasis Editions
Box 571
Banff, Alberta T0L 0C0

LIBRARY AND ARCHIVES CANADA CATALOGUING IN PUBLICATION

Levin, Dvora
    Sharav / Dvora Levin.

Poems.
ISBN 978-1-897430-17-0

    1. Israel--Poetry. 2. Spiritual life--Poetry. I. Title.

PS8623.E94782S53 2008   C811'.6   C2008-903389-2

Sharav has been published with the assistance of grants from the Canada Council for the Arts and the British Columbia Arts Council administered by the Cultural Services Branch of British Columbia.

Printed and bound in Canada.

Contents

Sharav:

Extremely hot dry weather brought by desert wind

*for my son
and his sons*

Ben Yehuda Promenade

The *sharav* has blown away all the voices.
Footsteps have melted into the cracks. Tonight,
only army uniforms pillar this place of gathering.
Doors cast their shadows into alleyways
and tearful windows slide along the walls,
their fingers chilled by the lonely wind.

In an empty café, I wait for a friend who does not come
and an unexpected one who does,
stuttering, "I just missed being exploded by minutes,
first here, then there,
so I cannot stay to eat.
Perhaps another time."

I sit with my foamy *café hafook* – upside down coffee,
alongside a young guard, armed with silence,
knowing he cannot protect himself or me,
only intermingle his fragments with mine
should it come to that.

I order a piece of apple cake,
nod to the invisible snake
as it slithers by
rippling the thick air.

Sand

As he was about to climb yet another dune, his heart whispered, "Be aware of the place where you are brought to tears. That's where I am, and that's where your treasure is."

The Alchemist, Paulo Coelho

Waiting

Imagine time as
ripples of sand formulating stillness,
an ancient desert well dug deep,
the lighthouse, disappeared with the freighter's passing.

Imagine time as
the waft of perfume held steady in a glass bottle,
letters vanished from fragments of parchment,
a robin painting its unborn eggs blue.

Imagine time as
the essence of being, curved without form,
continuous without space, and at its very centre,
a rose petal floating in a dry wind.

Mapping History

The lights dance over the rink.
The music plays. He takes
my arm, smiles and skates
on razor blades across my skin,
over my shoulders, down
the small of my back, over
buttocks, between thighs, criss-crossing
my ankle bones, between my toes,
and up again, cutting through belly scars,
road mapping my breasts,
slashing my nipples, and over
and down again, until
the thin ice over my heart
collapses with his weight
and he disappears under the melt.

Now I see only faded tracings,
vague twisting roads, cross-hatched rail lines
upon a map no longer current,
names no longer remembered,
places no longer visited.
Now when the music plays, I cross
the blue ice, my unskated face
lit by an opening and closing moon,
and glide.

A Few Things

She knows frost
        muffles the footfall,
        sugars holly berries,
        reveals the simple symmetry of shingles.

She knows Canada geese
        fly with the sound of a bored child
        swinging a squeaky door
        back and forth, back and forth.

She knows life
        is a series of rooms,
        each with an invisible door,
        misted windows.

What she doesn't know,
        can't be written
        even in a poem.

It can only be held in the *luminality* of sleep.

The Way of Woman

Budding breasts flower into roses,
entice roving tongues,
the rub of bumble beards,
then lie languid with milky nectar
to await the next coming.

Home at Dusk

Bamboo woven into chair,
silk thread into tapestry,
Sea grass woven into basket,
and you woven into me.

Purple woven into hills,
the flesh of trees into our library.
Between the covers, your cloven hooves
reverberate my pewter sea.

To My Valentine

Fill me with your honeyed musk.
Fill me with your unkempt lust.

Fill me with your hidden lure.
Fill me with your warming fur.

Fill me with your panther's arch.
Fill me with your mouth full parched.

Fill me with your blinded sight.
Fill me with your grazing bite.

Fill me with your rivered silt.
Fill me with your fecund milk.

If you love me, if at all,
Fill me with your silent howl.

And I,
I will be there.

Keeping Busy

"Are you having a busy day?" the store clerk asks with a smile.

I see busy bees buzzing, tethered at the end of frayed string,
machines chopping off the heads of chickens, plucked, cut,
rolled and fried golden nuggets grabbed from
"May I help you over here please" uniforms,
bolted by busy workers rushing back to busy e-mails,
voice-mails, faxes, meetings with busy bosses, then hurrying
to join the rush hour, car radios on busy news,
terrorism, train wrecks, busy bonds going up and down
to the bells of the stock exchange, arriving home
to answer voice mails, e-mails, snail mail, heating,
eating fast food while watching TV, talking on their cell phone.

Outside,
the last light dusts
a white chair
on a green lawn
above a sheen of water;
a single, white chair
empty,
suspended.

Remembering

A pebble knows it is mountain.
A spark knows it is fire.
A raindrop knows it is ocean.
Even a sigh knows it is wind.

Why do I forget I am God?

I don't mean the One gob-smacking
his children with curses, threats.
Nor do I mean the One in a chef's hat,
carefully ladling human soup
into white bowls and black bowls.
Nor do I mean the One perpetually soaked
with the sweat of forgiveness.

I mean, I forget I am the ineffable, luminous Essence of Being.

I forget I am riding a unicorn on a carousel,
rising and falling to the symphony
of expanding, exploding stars.
There is no ring to reach for.
Just to laugh as children laugh,
mouths sticky with the candy floss of wonder.

Everyone is there!
Everyone is riding!

Neighbours

Joseph lives next door
in a cottage built with his own hands.
It is white-washed and slightly sagging,
quiet and humble.

Like the Spartan apple tree in his yard,
Joseph is pruned small, round, with the soft sheen
of those "I can't use 'em all" apples
he hands me over the picket fence each fall.

While chatting one day, he said, "As a matter of fact,
my son was killed. He was only thirty-three."

In spring, my neighbour's garden is a cacophony,
trumpets of daffodils, drum sticks of grape hyacinth,
pink polyanthus pianos, tulips tooting up from the ground.
I often hear the slow clack clack of Joseph's push-mower
unrolling its carpet of apple green.

A neighbour once whispered to me,
 "They are Christians, practising I mean,
like goin' to church all the time and talking
about God and all that stuff,
fundamentalists, if you get my drift."

His wife, Mary's place is nearby,
her small garden a mirror of his, daffodils,
polyanthus, hyacinths, tulips, a carpet of green.
It's true there is a cross there, with her name
and a place for Joseph
when he is small enough
and quiet enough
to move in.

There is no place for their son.

Entry

Prophesy, visions and dreams,
cellophane that shimmers the everyday. If
you are still and very quiet, you can hear
the membrane cracking, see gray
shift to silver, to bronze, to gold.

I remember as a child walking home in the rain,
holding my tissue paper art against my sensible coat,
delighted when my coat shifted
into many colours, not caring
what they will say at home.

Now I study texts, commentaries that tell us
there are formulae at work:
        eleven levels of prophesy
        three kinds of dreams
        one dream equals one-sixtieth of a prophesy.

At the empty bus stop, I wait, read my books,
sift my thin visions, my half-forgotten dreams.
I wait for the translator, the one
who will tell me what everything means,
before, after it all happens.

I wait, longing
to get into
all that holy trouble.

Poet's Office

On a slippery dock, my notebook
falls out of my pocket into the lake.

The tail fin of a florescent fish I cannot name
whips me into fresh water.

I dive deep, sit upon the silty bottom
and write.

Suddenly

a poem will shiver the curtain,
reveal the opening,
offer a glimpse through
the glazed window;

as a song will,
or a prayer,
or your voice calling my name
suddenly.

Exception

Oh give me a poem
without the word bone,
without the word blood,
without the word stone.

No image of bird,
its claw, beak or wing.
Don't drag in stars, sun,
moon, the colour blue.

Unless it's a poem about Jackson Pollock,

This blue beaked bird claws
moon bone from the sun.
His drunken stoned wings
flick chaos into stars.

Escape

The cougar mist creeps across the lake,
low, intense, searching,
obscures the line between land and water.

The summer sun lurks behind the hills,
rifle at the ready. The hills bend
under the weight of the hunter.

I sit on the shore,
dissolving time and space,
prepared to duck the bullet.

Bronzed by first rays,
the elegant neck of a cormorant
glides by.

Advice

I saw you polishing your stone.
I threw in a little sand.
Life runs the grinder.

Master Cellist

for Claudio Ronco, Venetian Wanderer & Raconteur.

He holds her
    between his knees,
                resting, resting.

Caresses her slender neck,
    exposed throat,
                tending, tending.

Her elegant head
    leans into his shoulder,
                listening, listening.

His arm at her curved waist
    above her dark openings
                moving, moving.

Paired nakedness
    vibrate in unison
                coupling, coupling

and music cries out from their touching.

My Cellist

The bow lifts.
Silence contracts.
Everything is expectation,
a leaning into what is to come,
again and yet,
for the first time.

The opening note,
always a surprise,
an exquisite vibration;
like your voice in the dark
in our bed,
when your bow lifts.

Demolition

He put his hand under my dress,
and I,
I collapsed
under the pleasure.

The Hotel Room That Hums

*for Sister Margaret, founder of Oasis, a sacred space
in a downtown hotel for people of the street.*

Pass by the sign.
    No Noise After 11 PM
    Pay Rent On Time
    No Spitting

Climb the dark stairs. Unlock number eight.
Hot plate, one table, one couch, two chairs.
Plug in small waterfall. Light candle.
Place it before the centre poster,
two hands steepled in prayer.

Outside, noise.
Buses, trucks, car horns,
bikers astride their power glides,
crows, seagulls scream out
their raucous songs.

Inside,
five voices, five silences
transform darkness into light,
fear into love,
anger into forgiveness.

Outside drifts into dusk.
Inside halos into light,

The rustle of palm leaves in the desert wind.
Nomads gather, nibble plump, ripe dates.
The well dug so long ago, fills
with cool spring water.
The Oasis is singing.

Unplug the waterfall.
Blow out the candle.
Open the door.
Step into the night. Look!
Everyone is spitting,
spitting light.

Wife of a Hero

She lies peeled, wet, open,
languid with the heat,
and still you do not come.

Her eyes burn leaves as they fall.
Her mouth fills with rain, wind,
and still you do not come.

Fire-lit, quilted, she melts milk chocolate,
turn pages perfumed with Mozart,
and still you do not come.

The scent of lilac unfurls the evening news.
Afghanistan. Another flag-draped box. One more
year without you and still,

she keeps waiting,
keeps coming to you.

Dead Cat Bounce

On radio, the broker said,
when the market leaps on the down escalator
and investors panic, brokers mutter:
risk aversion, profit-taking. Then
a slight upturn on the Nasdaq, Dow Jones, TSX,
that time when greed and fear rumba side by side
not knowing if the escalator is going up or down,
that first little lift is called the dead cat bounce.
He explained, even a dead cat thrown from a height
will bounce a little, but never rise.

I remember Granny, bless her heart,
in that stuffy Old Folks Home,
all those Grannies with pink ribbons in their wispy hair.
The times we came, Granny gave us each a vacant smile,
asked who we were and why we there.
When we gathered round, right at the end
of Granny's eighty-eight well-sung years,
she grinned up at us and said our names in turn.
"Don't fret now," she said and died.
That was Granny's dead cat bounce.

And those marriages that sour over time,
how couples separate, and then,
that sudden cliché glimpse of him or her
across a crowded room, that so familiar smile,
exchanging funny stories of their time apart.
A glass of wine and they decide to reconcile,
try again, until they hear the counselor say:
"Your marriage needs lots of hard work."
Then they know they've just jived
the dead cat bounce.

Announcing new peace talks in the Middle East,
analysts say there is little chance of success.
The American Secretary of State with her flashbulb smile,
thirty staff, briefcases. The Israeli Prime Minster shakes
her hand. She drinks tea with the Chairman of Palestine.
The agenda is agreed upon, borders, prisoners, refugees.
Jerusalem will be left to last. King David's camp in the woods,
opening ceremonies full of possibility. Within a day or two,
sometimes four or five, talks break down. Planes arrive
to retrieve another dead cat thrown from a great height.

Living Small

There is a man,
neither old nor young,
who lives in a room in a basement.

The room is small.
The house is old,
in a sagging street in Belgrade.

He lies on a bed,
red wine in a cup
on a table stacked with books.

There is one wooden chair.
He listens in his room
for the small boy's tap on the door.

How often they sit,
a cup of wine, a cup of milk,
speaking lines from his books,

of the soiled jacket that hangs
on the back of the door,
the jacket that Hemingway left

in Cuba one day,
in a run down café,
a place where his sister had worked.

She sent it to him.
He never heard more.
She left so long ago.

He sees the boy grow,
gives him tea in a cup,
watches him move away.

The soiled jacket he folds,
puts into a box,
with a pencil he writes the boy's name.

The man tidies his books,
takes a rope and the chair,
opens the door to the courtyard.

Yes, there is a man
who lives alone,
with Hemingway's jacket in Belgrade,

in a room too small for hanging.

Island Winter

Skeleton trees wave their thin arms,
remind us they are alive, arteries pulsing.

A bare finger displays a nest ring,
invites the fragility of egg.

The simple symphony of wind.
oscillates winter grays.

On distant mountains, snow magnolias
blossom, melt and blossom again.

The ocean, a slate roof,
freighters sledding across its shingles.

Unseen below, great rifts, cracks that seethe heat,
lava , unimagined winged creatures; reveal

the broken eggshell we all float upon.
In this shrink of dark, we solitudes mushroom

the city streets, disappear and reappear.
Like drops of rain, flakes of snow, we shift

between liquid and solid. Inside, we nest
on painted pillows, Persian rugs. Warmed

by the fire, we float naked in candle light,
imagining the embroidered spring.

Portrait of Kirsti

You tell me you see everything double,
one image and its duplicate beside,
You say: "I see you there in front of me,
and another you beside, and superimposed
on you, is that file cabinet."

It is your hair, I first ask about, that pale
sheaf of wheat falling to your waist.
Smoothing it with your hand, you tell me
you never cut it since that day,
such a blessing it had all grown back.

There were four of you in the car that day,
four sisters and then there were three. With fragments
of skull pushed into your brain, three broken vertebrae,
your parents are given the gift of inventory:
> If she lives, she may never wake up.
> If she wakes up, she may never walk,
> may never see, never hear,
> never know you or herself again.

Each day, your parents, two sisters arrive to hold your hand,
speak of everyday things and pray. The nurse
calls out for the doctor, you standing there tidying
the table beside the bed, four and a half months gone
and things to do. Your first question,
"What happened to Lena?" Somehow you knew.

It isn't that they were completely wrong.
You do walk but in a shadow of pain.
You do hear but only from one ear,
see a little from the eye that melts down your face.

Everyday you carry a basket of simple joy.
"You see, God is always with me", you say.
Sampsoness, you sit at the reception desk,
tidying papers, tapping on the computer,
one eye looking off into its own corner.

I say, "Since you see everything double,
always two of everything,
nothing itself, nothing separate alongside,
how do you know which is real,
my *doppelganger* or me,
and what about that God of yours
and that God standing beside?
You smile, softly say, "I always know which one is real."

Trailing all that is superimposed,
all that is beside the point,
I turn and walk my selves away.

Weapons Training I

In Miss Kimball's class, since I was good
in arithmetic, spelling and comportment,
I was sent to the office to get the strap
for Billy, Frank or Tommy.
We all knew the strap was for boys.
When Miss Kimball raised her voice,
we girls cringed,
did everything she said.

Most times, Miss Kimball preferred to strap
that big kid she called "Johnny-come-lately".
Late for school two or three times a week,
Johnny would slouch in, shirttail hanging,
buttons undone or long gone.
All we knew: he had a fat mom,
five brothers, a dumpy house,
hands like wedges of cheese.

Prim Miss Kimball let that thick leather tongue
"do all the talking".
She could hit the tips of fingers
so they would burn for hours,
make even the toughest boys cry.
Johnny never blinked an eye,
just stood there and took it,
ten whacks, five on each hand.

Walking the long, empty hall to return the strap,
I felt relief, maybe a kind of stain.
Who knows what a child feels watching
Miss Kimball's smirk and that strange glitter in her eyes?

I never once looked into Johnny's face,
never said a word to him. The next year,
he was gone.

Weapons Training II

Decades later, as I walk down my long hallway,
I think about my good girl life:

briefcase stuffed with child welfare files,
drug addicts kidnapped for counseling,
money management workshops for the poor,
mediation training for Palestinian/Israeli security,
strategic plans for understaffed police.

I remember that glitter in Miss Kimball's eyes
and ask myself: What did I do?   What did I say?

Please, strap me instead of Johnny.
Let's just run those burning fingers under cold water, take your pain away.
Did I hand the strap to some executive smirker to display his expertise,
or in my mind say, What strap? I don't see any strap.
Did I say okay, here's the strap, but only one light whack on each hand,
or I suggest you strap that one over there, sir.
Did I ever say, No way! Go get your own strap
or drop the strap down the garbage shute?
Was I the one wielding the strap?
Was I the strap itself?

My mind burns. Ten whacks,
each one reeking of yes,
that too. I did that too.

Preemptive Strike

Winter in the Canadian Rockies.
Climax avalanches strike without warning.

Road crews aim air-pressured Howitzers
anchored to metal footings,
shoot at the steep slopes,
remove the snow.

Heavy equipment always at the ready,
should icy slides and dangerous rock
try to take out the road,
block the flow of travelers.

Now, that's my kind of war!

Junkie Jesus: Life of a Cop

for Deputy Chief Bill Naughton, Victoria Police Department

You boogie in the belly of the beast,
       gettin' high on doin' good.
            It's the rush that keeps you in.

Working neon streets, you're at home
       on hookers stroll, call dealers "bro".
            You dig pig farmers who specialize, customize.

Your cool shades flick at empty doors,
       vinyl booths in fried cafés,
            pinball eyes passing in the park.

You find a way to feed the multitudes,
       your own bones, ground up fine,
            crusts of bread, without the wine.

When they want you, they want you bad
       they want you fast,
            then they want you gone.

You know the time may come when Judas pawns his kiss,
       for a knife, or a gun,
            you are whacked if it comes to that.

You keep all options open
       all but one, that's to lose,
            go down once and you are through.

Crucified by hate, you give and take all bad news,
       you hit the bars, do couch time,
            pay someone to pretend to care.

Those night-shift hours slide along,
        repel the dawn. Sometimes you hear
                lice moving on the moon.

This movie reels, again and again as you nail
        on your badge, tuck in those well-pressed blues,
                and rise
                        one more time.

The Swimmer

for Ben

He says the best way not to be eaten by a shark;
be sure you are not the furthest one out.

He says he was a one-man crime wave, a small businessman
adept at finding a new niche in the market,
stealing twelve hundred dollars a day
from parking meters, laundry rooms, a master
lock-picker, key-maker high on crystal meth
for seven years
when not in jail.

On probation, drug-free, he says he must
repay, rebalance his world. Free of charge,
he advises businessmen on security –
	the best locks,
	theft of identity,
	positioning video cameras,
	how to catch drugged-up thieves.

He works for the parking firm he stole
thirty thousand dollars from, a promise kept
by the owner were this thief to decide to straighten
out his corkscrew life. He earns sixty dollars a day.

Now, sleek, fit, articulate,
each chilly morning, he reaches
right arm, left arm, breathes in,
stroke, stroke, breathes out,
reaches right arm, left arm;
attempting to perfect his crawl,

his thin fin barely visible from the distant shore.

The Plum Party

In the singing sun, we have come to plum
the tree of the bungalow on Harbinger Street,
this great Pavarotti tree, tall and broad,
its profusion of plump notes hanging in the air;
not the dark purple plums of the baritone,
but the golden orbs of the tenor, delicious
and sweet as Luciano's renown high Cs.

At two on a Sunday afternoon, friends gather.
Puccini's aria, *Nessun Dorma,* pours from the window,
trembles the grass, as we sip sparkling wine and tea,
share plum recipes, jams, chutneys, tarts, upside-down cake.
The lower branches are easily picked.
The wooden ladder, unstable on uneven ground,
cannot reach high enough. Someone has brought a long pole
with a cup on top, for changing light bulbs in high ceilings,
he explains, as he deftly plucks the topmost notes.

We fill our bowls, bags, pockets, ourselves to the brim.
We see the great tree has dimmed its lights,
its leafy cape made plain, unadorned.
A silence sets in, and a chill.
A few unreachable plums turn amber in the setting sun.
Guests drift home to display, devour, do up plum preserves.

We hear Pavorotti has died; our plum party, a harbinger.
Our Olympic Prince, vanished in the cold night.
His star has set. No one shall sleep.
He leaves his preserves, golden juicy CDs.
The flutter of his white handkerchief, silk scarf,
his full-belly smile, all over-large,
all lost, all disappeared.

With all those yellow plums we picked, surely one pit,
maybe more, will be tossed during a concert on the lawn,
to fall on fertile ground, take root, and when the light shines,
become another Pavorotti tree, a great cape adorned
with golden tenor plumbs and yes,
those round, sweet high Cs.

And You

Lodge pole pine
Calling loon

Velvet light
Quarter moon

Rain drop lake
Lac Le Jeune

Buddhist Life

Off cliff falling.
Berry bush grabbing.
Weighted roots wrenching.
One berry plucking.
Doomed body dropping.
Just before crashing,
red ripe berry
into mouth popping.

Ah, delicious!

Wind

Deep calls to deep in the roar of Your torrents;
All your breakers and billows overwhelm me.
                              Psalm 42

Jerusalem Lover

Your palms reach up to open dusk,
as lamps cream the stone, light
the darkening from beneath and ah yes,
those dates, oblong clusters licked
by the sun, ripening thick and dark
and you, there with your muscled thighs,
hot breath, meticulous tongue.

Unframed sepia:
The *hamsin* wind sanding my eyes.
Your musk on my wrists.
A hint of jasmine.
Salt on my fingers.
The taste of ripe date in my bruised mouth.
A small pit, hard in my palm.

Military Handbook

On the dangerous back of Jerusalem,
tufts of green spring between the massive thighs,
the Judean Hills roll down to Jericho,
down to the deepest place on Earth.

Overhead, the acute sky is cut
by icy parabolas, tracks of jet fighters
scanning for movement;
for hot sand trying to be glass.

A sign at the crest of the long descent:

Warning!
  Stay in low gear.
  Check your brakes.
  Safety ramp ahead.

Off to the side of the paved road, the ramp –
a narrow dirt path, dead-ended by a spindly, wire fence
at the edge of a deep ravine,
compelling a full stop in time.

The Bent Nail

At Zion gate the light catches her. Its cream
thickened by the day, holds her in place.
The wall is dusted with pink, the inexplicable
pastels of Jerusalem stone
stacked block upon block.

She touches its warm face, pocked
by desert sands, smeared
with the curses of prophets hawking our doom.
Even now, their thin green fingers reach out
between the widening cracks.

She leans into the stone. In the dirt,
newspapers crumple with new prophesies,
orange peels shrivel the dreams of Jaffa, Jericho,
used condoms stop forbidden seed from spilling into the dust.

Then,
          the muezzin calls…
                              The light shifts.

She hears the rock inhale, exhale
the arch – the opening.
The entrance is a hard right angle,
making swift entry impossible.

Here she knows
the shape of things,
the breath of stone,
the path is bent.

Our Eclipse

There is a legend of lovers cursed.
By night, he became wolf. She was woman.
By day, she became hawk. He was man.
Each dawn, each twilight, for one anguished moment,
they could almost touch, as humans, as lovers.
Then the agony of transformation,
he into wild wolf, she into wild hawk,
again and again. The curse
to be broken only when a rare eclipse
turns day into night, night into day.

Now our stage stretches across half the world,
the sorcerer earth spins your day into my night,
my day into your night. You are the wolf
who hunts me in the dark, and I,
I have become the hawk who must fly
through the eclipsed sky to make
my day, your day,
your night, my night.

When you stroke my tired wings and speak
my Hebrew name which means "honey bee",
I become woman.
When I lean into your warm fur and speak
your name which means "my strength",
you become man.

Lips touch eyelids and we see
the same transparency.
At dawn, your breath dresses me in gossamer,
blushed Jerusalem pink and cream.
At twilight, your fingers weave
desert feathers in my hair. We dance
to the music we have just composed.
Your sinewed hands around my waist, you lift.
I arch above your head.

My wings curve in the shifting light and
I soar above the Rockies to fly once more
with ravens, seagulls, pods of killer whales,
while you continue to repair
Jerusalem's breached and broken walls.

As we dance our duet of separate destinies,
we are always almost touching.

*The Kotel**

I press my forehead to your stone face.
You do not give way.
My flesh gives way
only to the bone of my skull.

My fingers grope for a handhold
between your veins stuffed
with small prayer scrolls.
We know we are both wearing away.

What is there in this meeting?

Our touch, warm
in the cool of night,
cool in the heat of day.
A moment of joining

without resistance,
without expectation,
together as our cells slough off
and drift invisible to the earth.

* *Western* Wall of the Temple Mount in Jerusalem

Ownership

This is the place I've been drawn to,
this rough fabric, its pockets stuffed with prayers,
this Wall.

It is ours.

My fingers feel the heat of the day
held a little longer, as we are, by this stone.
I stand small in this small place, know the border,
this seam between above and below, is savagely rent,
a gaping armhole in the tight jacket so badly constructed
by those British tailors, after the Second World War.

Each spring, frail white blossoms appear between the cracks.
Black hats with side curls, their foreheads pale,
eyes glistening, black and white prayers shawls
bob and weave muttering
Adonai, Eloheem.

He is ours.

At the torn shoulder, a ramp, a narrow
path curves upwards. A gate.
Since my arms are bare, I am given
a dusty *gallabiah* to wear. There is no hood.
Through the gate, the Golden Dome of the Rock,

It is theirs.

At the Al Aksa Mosque, a scatter of shoes,
mustached men bend at water spouts, rinse
thin ankles, wrists and necks, touch
knees, foreheads to ornate carpets,
genuflect to *Allah.*

He is theirs.

Beside the Mosque, a small museum.
I see it is open today, free of charge.
I step inside, briefly blinded by the shift in light.
And there they are, blood stained T-shirts,
seventeen of them pinned to the wall.

I wonder at the soft brown that blood becomes.
There are photos too, martyrs
they are called on the plaque,
these young faces looking out with a kind of pride,
except for this one. He looks older, sadder.
Their deaths during that 1990 riot on the Temple Mount,
that mad time of throwing stones,

That was them.

tear gas and bullets

That was us.

Suddenly, sirens mass on Jaffa Road.
I am asked to leave.
They will close early today. Polite.
Later I hear a bomb was found.

That was them.

I feel the stone, the steel,
this fabric bleached hard and thin.
I see his arm, my arm are bound,
long straps wound round and round
strapped inside one tattered straight jacket.

It is theirs.
It is ours.
It is mine.

Jerusalem, Holy Cup of Gold,
flattened by myriad clichés,
thrusts upon us a throbbing
energy so great, it cuts
clean through the
crackling static
of the mind
to broadcast
inexplicable
joy and awful violence;
a broad-banded radiation station
linked eternal to the soul-force satellite.

Your Wailing Wall

for Avram

This stone wall is not your foundation,
your fence, nor your gate.
It is a refection of you.

Wings of doves agitate the air
and your every empty space is filled
with the same love prayer.

Your skin, touched by so many hands,
some delicate, some desperate, their absence
brings such persistent longing.

Your wall is so often broken
by that earthquake, that uproar
of falling in love.

All your carefully hewn, stacked stones
tumble into chaos, into ecstasy,
quickly followed by

the settling,
the turning away,
the awful silence,
rubble and dust,

and you waiting there
to be put together again,
reconstructed into any shape
that can be recognized.

Palestinian Shop in Jenin

Summer heat.   Oranges.
Forty days on duty.   The Israeli soldier is thirsty.
The shopkeeper refuses service; hears the click
of the soldier's bullet as it enters the chamber.

A chipped glass slapped on the counter.
Each orange sliced in two.
The metal hand-press squeezes.
The juice, that a moment ago
was not there, in that place,
for him or his kind,
ever again,
appears.

Warm flesh made liquid
by an eighteen year old's threat.

Twenty years later, on Yom Kippur *
the soldier, speaking in Victoria,
tells his story; knows
he needs forgiveness.

Ten thousand miles. Twenty years of thirst
and this splintered moment reappears.
An opening.
An altar.   In Jenin,

the old shopkeeper slumps on his stool.
Summer heat.   Soldiers.
In one hand he holds a picture
of his dead son, in the other,
an orange.

Day of Atonement

Warriors

Seeds press up against
the dry skin of the Negev.

A brief rain.
Poppies!

Red flags hoisted to a history
sliced by war.

Red, so frantic it cannot last.
Red, so fervent it must return.

This Time in the Land

The clock is falling off the page. All the numbers
are gone and only one hand showing.
The moon has wasted to a sliver
and I no longer sleep through the night.

Like a plague of locusts,
tanks infest the towns
to forage for bombers,
fueled for swift ascension.

Of the ten plagues,
locusts were the eighth,
followed by darkness,
then, the unconscionable slaying of the first born.

Again, the locusts.
Again, the darkness.
Again, blood on the lintels.
This time the first born on both sides are dying.

This time, a ruthless summer has blossomed
flowers of metal,
fragments of bone,
again, a dark red rain.

No doubt, one day, a pall of peace will settle,
but the wine will be down to the dregs.
The plates will be scattered.
Many of the chairs will be empty.

A Third Option

Moslems say Moses died in *Nebe Musa,*
on the West Bank of the Jordan;
was tucked into the Judean hills.
His kiss-encrusted tomb now lies
in a blue domed mosque, its garden littered
with graves of the faithful who followed.

Jews say he did not cross into the promised land.
After leading his people out of slavery,
through forty years in the desert, he was allowed
only to stand on the threshold, punished
for the slightest of sins
by that fiercest of Commanders.

I say perhaps Moses took a Chagall flight to peek
at the next chapters, when some ancient Arab
goat herder spotted him flying by,
and where he still appears on occasion,
with his blue violin and red cow,
to nurture the fanatics and the faithful alike.

Israeli Independence Day (2002 C.E.)

On the winding road to Jerusalem, each lamppost sprouts
brief wings, blue star ribbons
to mark the breach birth of a state
on that momentous day over half a century ago.

Once flown by ecstatic winds, this spring
these faded flags are waved by thin, exhausted arms,
while the wind scurries among the ruins
looking for a way out.

Diplomacy

The arm wielding the knife hangs limp
from the ripped-out shoulder, one fierce red eye
straining to see if the hand is open or clenched.

In a far away land, foreign physicians
in clean white coats, clutch overexposed x-rays,
huddle to discuss the treatment.

Clever surgeons, crowded with consequence,
recommend the clean cut of amputation,
hidden burial of the afflicted limb.

In a dirty surgery, local doctors, muddled
with forgetfulness, thread their thick needles
for the stitching, without anesthetic, in a fading light,

knowing the chances of infection, death;
the ghost arm reaching not for a plowshare,
but a gun.

Negotiations

*Dedicated to the Joint Team of Israeli and Palestinian negotiators during
the standoff between the Israeli Defense Forces and the Palestinians
encamped in the Bethlehem's Church of the Nativity [April, 2002]*

I

Nuns, priests and policemen held hostage
as Palestinian gunmen hot-wire
the manger of baby Jesus, proclaim
their desired ascension into innocence.
Outside, the armored children of the chosen
are nailed to their tanks.

Yet what choosing do these chosen have
encircling such a resurrection?
There are rumours of stolen crucifixes.
On the roof a sign waving, *Save Us,*
staccato gun shots, one man beaten,
two bodies carried to the gate.

Outside the circle, soothsayers sit cross-legged
in canvas tents, warrior nomads
count the hairs of an aging camel,
search the cloudless sky
for the words of a prophet,
for one drop of mystical rain.

The first agreement, the nuns are permitted to leave.
They refuse, boil water, make tea and pray.

II

After thirty-eight days, it's over. This morning,
we hear on the radio the tanks have crawled
back to their caves, leaving the narrow alleyways
infected with their rumblings.

It is agreed the gunmen will be scattered,
a few to the dense ditch of Gaza,
a few to the steepled streets of Europe.
Each side claims victory.

Released into the day, eyes bleached white,
ragged nuns and priests drop to their knees,
press their cracked lips to the sacred ground.
Drops of morning dew already disappeared.

Collateral Damage - Funeral in Beit Zeit

Twenty-two hours after the death of a young mother,
we gather at the top of the hill, walk
silent behind a grey van, on pavement,
then on rough stone, down to the smooth stones
carved with names and dates,
down to the valley of shadow.

Clouds curtain the light.
Between sentinel evergreens, we stand
with her soldier father, soldier husband,
a son too young to serve. We know
our grief will one day be leaving,
and she will not.

A small black dog circles the crowd
and the weeping. Armed guards sit
cross-legged on the jeep, too late to halt
a mother's death, when her anxious thoughts
plowed her car into a stalled tank truck
that was too laden to move forward.

After the amens, alone,
her husband crouches beside her
to whisper his first goodbye.

Middle East Circus

In centre ring, trapeze artists
practice their amazing acrobatics.
Israelis, arms frozen to remote smoke stacks,
hang upside down to catch.
Palestinians, exhausted by insoluble dreams,
poised aloft to leap.

Their rigging flaccid with the heat,
their safety net rotted beyond despair,
in a constant acid rain,
both are determined
to do the impossible;
to fly between the drops.

On the midway, villagers and soldiers from both sides
cheer on their local strong-arm to ring the bell.
The most popular event, the coin toss,
where media and experts gather to lay bets,
heads or tails, on who will be victim,
who will be victimizer this week.

At night, circus-goers lie in their thin beds,
dream of flying solo,
of ringing the bell,
of winning the last game.
At dawn, they line up to buy tickets
for the next carnival coming to town.

Caesarea

In the spring sunlight, a small wooden table,
white linen cloth held down
by silver spoons and sparkling water.
On the shore of the Mediterranean,
we sit together, silent among these blocks,
porous rocks, hewn, stacked and re-stacked,

first by Romans, then Crusaders,
followed by your Moslems, now my Jews.
Each conqueror rebuilds the wall,
raises a tower, digs a moat,
to protect borders briefly owned,
never held.

Moon-tugged waves alternately flog
and caress the shore, grind the rock,
smooth the sand. The turquoise sea whispers
incantations to its ancient harbour,
its constant borders
always held.

We eat slowly, watch
two fisherman cast their lines,
again and again,
and then once more,
to take one fish at a time,
not to disturb the quiet order.

Neshamah

*The Government of Israel has built a fence between their land and
the land of the Palestinians to protect themselves against attack.*

The man bends, scoops mortar onto a thin trowel,
stands, spreads it, careful.
Lifts, places a cement block on top,
taps it in place, gentle.

Gray mortar between gray blocks.
The fence.   A wall.

The man straightens. Heat burns his face.
He turns toward the hills, weary,
looks for a sign of a breeze,
a prophesy.

Forty meters away, a Palestinian boy sits
on his haunches, grasshopper legs
poke out of ragged pants.
Nearby, a herd of dusty goats.

The boy's soft stare catches the man's throat,
stops up his breath.

Do you know the Hebrew word for breath
has the same root as the word for soul – *Neshamah?*

The man scrapes the seam smooth,
reaches for another block.
The boy turns his head, looks
toward the empty hills.

Along the wall, an army tractor heaves into sight,
its iron fingers draw thin, straight lines on flat soil.
Israeli Bedouin trackers wait in the shade
for a footprint to appear.

Beyond the hills, in Jerusalem,
an explosion.

The man wipes his face with his frayed hat.
The boy stares.   The goats huddle.

*Silent Thrumming at the Edge of the Universe**

You have left Your place, left the harp beat
of angels' wings, stepped out of Ezekiel's chariot
to climb down Jacob's ladder
in search of an opening
to explode Your vastness
and retrieve Your fame.

Now Lord, Master, King of the Universe,
You lurk in alleyways, Your molten eyes wrapped
in a black and white *kafiah.***
You crouch, tightening the blades on backhoes
to crush the homes of the poor.
You generate precision bombing at five thousand feet,
find stones to fit the fist of a child.

Your name appears so often
in cafés, at airports, in tattered fields,
on buses and in busy streets.
With so many worshippers clutching
at Your club feet, You stumble,
as a drunken beggar stumbles,
starving and in retreat.

* Elizabeth Brewster
** Arab man's head scarf

Two Poets Meet

In the middle of the night, the taxi came.
The Arab driver and I waited
while you collected your bags.

Looking up, I spoke my poem:
Hard white, upright, half moon
slips down into a begging bowl.

The Arab driver spoke his poem:
It looks like a banana, he said.

Respite

A snowfall in Jerusalem lightens the air,
plants a carrot nose, cherry tomato eyes,
pine tree hair, gives miraculous
birth to a desert snowman.

At the first flake, everyone rushes from work, school,
the cafés, to bask in the startled light.
Each breath can be counted.
Each sound, a singular note.

This rare whiteness separates
the before and the after,
as the white space that separates
the endless commentaries.

Snow brings a strange quietude
before that unremitting pipe organ,
that calico choir,
strike up again.

Acknowledgements

With gratitude to Patrick Lane, poet extraordinaire, and fellow poets at Glenairlie retreats and Planet Earth Poetry; the many friends in Israel who enhance my journey with such love and wisdom; and Richard Olafson and Carol Ann Sokoloff at Ekstasis Editions, who helped shape this vessel.

Dvora Levin is a vessel, thinning her clay through poetry, to reveal more of her light. A regular reader at Planet Earth Poetry in Victoria, BC, she has published the chapbooks, *To Bite the Blue Apple: Healing Poems* (Ekstasis Editions) and *This Time in the Land,* as well as poems in five chapbooks edited by Patrick Lane (Leaf Press). She has read poems on CBC Radio and participated in the Poet Tree Project. She leads poetry writing workshops in the workplace and for people of the street.

As a project manager and management consultant, Dvora has shared her vessel with governments in the province of British Columbia and in Israel, as well as the University of Victoria and the Victoria Police Department. She worked for thirteen years in Jerusalem, in the fields of tolerance and conflict resolution, including joint training of Israeli and Palestinian Security Forces. She is on the executive of Victoria's heritage synagogue, having served as Cemetary Director and President. Currently, she lives in a small box with a big view of the Strait of Juan de Fuca and the Olympic Mountains, working with leaders and executives in the process of rewiring their lives.